MERRY CHRISTMAS

1974

Bill Laughlin

By SOLAR FORST

With Decorations by

PAT STEWART

THE PETER PAUPER PRESS

Mount Vernon, New York

Prefatory Note

Lost among the billions of planets in our galaxy, among the planets of the entire universe, trembles a tiny grain of dust which is called man.

In his human soul and heart he is concerned with "I" rather than the vast, unending space of the universe. And every one of those insignificant, unimportant "I's" in the midst of his burdensome life stops for a moment and asks: "Why?" Thousands of poets, philosophers and prophets over thousands of years have tried to answer. The author of this little book is not trying to solve the mystery of life, but wants only to recount a few personal experiences which although sometimes very difficult, were in the over-all picture, beautiful and happy!

The author wants to say to all harassed and bitter people, that one thing above all is of the utmost importance: to keep pure of heart, to retain the world of childhood, to glow with the magic of Christmas all year round; to burn with love and joy and transmit happiness to others; to know how to love and how to laugh, to take simple pleasure from the falling snow, from the rain and from sunshine; to enjoy the dandelions in a spring meadow and the golden leaves in the autumn. And not to know hate, envy or wrath!

William Ellery Channing painted the picture in a few well-chosen words: "To live content with small means, to seek elegance rather than luxury and refinement rather than fashion; to be worthy, not respectable, wealthy, not rich: to study hard, think quietly, talk frankly, to listen to the stars and birds, to babes and sages with open heart; to bear adversity cheerfully, do all bravely, await events patiently, make haste never; in a word, to let the spiritual, unexpected and unconsciousness grow up through the common; this is to be my symphony."

The Alphabet of Life

THE ALPHABET OF LIFE

Advent

O yes, we are living in advent.

We are waiting for the coming of the Saviour.

The Just One, sans discrimination, loving all people, all colors, all nations, all religions, all classes!

Advice

In giving advice, seek to help, not to please your friend.   SOLON

Aim

Tell me what is your aim in life and I will tell you who you are.

Tell me your motto!

Tell me to what your heart is dedicated, tell me your interests!

Do not aim low!

Find your star, your Stella Polaris.

Amen

We await the Kingdom of love and peace! the Kingdom of understanding and tolerance! the Kingdom of respect of one man to another! AMEN!

Apostle

There are no apostles any more!

What would they do among automobiles and jets, in our time of go-go and television?

How far you are from us, you apostles of old, you simple fishermen with the pure hearts of children, loving and believing!

Architect

You build our houses, you build our domes and bridges, but where are the architects of our hearts and souls?

Where are the architects who build the bridges between one man and another? Between nation and nation?

Ball

No edge, no angle, no beginning, no end. No privileges, no patronage nor discrimination. But what beautiful resilience!

Black Cat

Never search in the darkness of night for a black cat which is not there!

Bravery

Courage!
Determination!
Patience!

Breathing

How much optimism, how much joy there is in the simple saying of Papini: "Breathing is the greatest pleasure in life."

How little we appreciate the fact that we are able to breathe. It is for us a natural function without meaning.

How little we actually treasure the gift of fresh air is shown by the amount of industrial air pollution and the consumption of countless cigarettes.

Is there some connection between fresh air and a fresh spirit?

Cannon

On an old cannon was engraved:
"The final argument of kings."

A good piece of engraving but a bad argument!

Nothing lasting, eternal or essential was ever achieved by war.

The greatest human problems are solved by the intellect and the heart, not by cannons and bayonets.

Character

It has been said that man's character is his fate.

It does not matter who you are, or whether your name is in the social register —

What matters is your heart!

Choice

Every man should be his own Christopher Columbus.

EMIL FAGUET

To find your right place in the world, your own field, your own garden or your own work involves a very serious and difficult choice.

Debts

We all have debts — to our parents, to our teachers, to our nation, to our people.

We are in debt to nature for the beauty of the mountains, the forests and the sea; for the beauty of sunrise and the loveliness of a starry night.

We are in debt to the poets — the poets of words, paint and music.

We have many debts — debts without end!

Diamond in the Rough

Those who can appraise people rightly, give preference to the rough, coarse and uncouth instead of the glib, smooth and sugary.

Let us not be deceived and discouraged by a rough surface. Let us examine the core.

The core is what counts — the core!

Discipline

Discipline is for every man what the two banks are for a river.

Don't

Worry!

Enthusiasm

Your soul is like an automobile tire, which instead of the right amount of air must have the right amount of enthusiasm and love, humor and good will — otherwise the road will be lonely and bumpy.

Eternity

Life — *sub specie aeternitatis!*

For some, eternity is too much —

For those people, I have this advice:

Live with the thought of your own end ever-present. Joyful is the spectacle of a man who is enthusiastic and dedicated, — who reaches beyond and above!

He reaches toward eternity!

Every Man

"Every Man" is like a lamp giving us light with which to see ourselves, — a bridge to the knowledge of who we are!

Facts

We should verify and then honor them — we should not be afraid of them — we should look them straight in the eye and not distort them.

Our principle should be the one most honored by journalists the world over: *Comments are free, facts are sacred!*

Falseness

Falseness is a sign of weakness, cowardice, of shortsighted selfishness which speculates in human frailty.

Falseness, like a lie, has short legs — it cannot walk very far.

But it can cause a great deal of damage!

Fatalism

Waiting for what life will bring — God knows what's best for us — We just have to be patient —

No, no, my friends!

He who has blood, and not water, in his veins will not give up — he will fight.

. . . And when sometimes the circumstances are stronger than he, he waits, gathering his strength for the next life-battle.

Faults

*Think about your own faults before you fall
asleep, and about the faults of others when you
are sleeping.*

CHINESE PROVERB

Fear

There is an old Hindu fable:

A traveler one day met Death on a road. He
asked her whither she was hurrying.

Death answered that she had been sent to kill
fifty thousand people by the plague.

After some time the traveler met Death again.
Reproachfully he said to her: "You did not keep
your word. You were supposed to kill fifty
thousand people but you killed a hundred and
fifty thousand."

Answered Death: "I killed fifty thousand people
with the plague. The other hundred thousand
died of fear."

Filter

A filter is a piece of equipment which cleans the impurities from our water, so we can drink it.

We all should filter everything that comes our way: news, gossip, books and television — we should allow only the beautiful and pure to approach our souls.

Why don't we leave all the dirt and vulgarity out on the doorstep?

Finish

In medieval ages the moralists pondered upon the last days of their lives.

But most people do not like to dwell upon the closing chapters of their lives, — the departure.

During an illness or at a friend's funeral, we will give it passing thought. But mostly we shrug our shoulders: "Who wants to think about death?"

Well, we do not really need to think about

death, — just about the approach of old age.

We need to think and be ready.

Fools

Few things characterize a man better than the way he handles fools.

Forgiveness

Learn how to forgive!

Do not store up forever all the offenses and insults you have received in days gone by.

The head and heart are made for better things than to be archives of angry words some unhappy person poured out upon us. Besides, lack of forgiveness spoils the digestion!

Form

How often we overlook and sneer at it!

More often, we tend to overestimate it! We are

deceived by a pretty face, good manners, a glib tongue. To find the right substance and give it a natural and suitable form is one of the most difficult and most rewarding things in life.

Future

The future is a blank page.

It will be what you write upon it.

Gift

To know how to give is a rare art.

An even rarer and greater art is to know how to receive; to know how to be grateful.

A good word, a kind smile, can be a gift.

Giving

However much we give, that much shall be returned to us.

In the last analysis, the world is quite just.

Goodness

In today's greedy and grasping times goodness has almost become a mockery.

A "good" man is one who is given the work nobody else is willing to do; he is made the scapegoat and his life is not an easy one.

The word "good," just as the word "virtue," is becoming obsolete. And yet, on the shoulders of the good, stands the whole world.

The good are the salt of the earth, the conscience of the world and the sunshine of those around them.

The good ones are wise — they do not know envy, hate or wrath.

They make no judgments; they just understand and forgive.

Gratitude

We are strange! We like to be praised but we do not like to praise!

We like to be thanked but we do not like to thank others.

We expect gratitude and we are so little grateful.

We like to get letters but we do not like to answer them.

Is it because we cannot truly place ourselves in the other person's shoes?

Hand

The hand is the symbol of humanity, of love, of brotherhood, of promise. The fist is the symbol of war, hatred and cruelty. The palm of the hand denotes peace, friendship, understanding and forgiveness.

Humanity, sick and ailing, will be cured not by a fist but by a friendly open hand.

Happiness

Happiness is not a sack full of money.

Happiness is not a palace full of treasure.

Happiness is a heart full of sunshine, and of good will, — a heart full of love!

Hate

Perhaps our great great grandson will ask his father: "Can you tell me the meaning of the word 'hate'? I came across it, by chance, in a very old book!"

Heart

Kindness

Joyfulness

Tolerance

Heritage

A man should value two things: First, the labor of those who came before us, those who planted the orchards which we are harvesting now, those who built the roads we use today and the houses we live in, and those who wrote books and composed music which give us strength and joy.

The other thing?

yourself what kind of heritage you will leave to those who come after you.

That is what matters!

History

No science can give us such a summary of world events, such penetration into the souls of humanity as can history.

No science can disillusion us and at the same time imbue us with as much faith and trust in mankind. Come what may, history should teach us to keep our feet planted firmly on the ground.

Home

Home is security, certainty, peace, comfort, relaxation.

It is the place where we can find each and every doorknob in the dark!

How L___

___ll we live? How long will our
___w long shall we be as well off

as we are now? Two thousand years ago Cice
said: "Nobody is so old that he does not hope
for at least another year."

Why don't we sometimes stop for a moment on
a busy day and ask ourselves: "Is it wise to be
angry, to get excited over a trifling matter, over
a broken shoe-lace, spilled milk, a missed train
or a rainy weekend?"

How long will it be remembered?

g

Each of us has two "I's":

"I" — impulsive, primitive, selfish, low.

"I" — pure, rich, human, disciplined.

The two "I's" battle within us from the first
days of our childhood; from the first "you must"
and "you must not."

Blessed is he who can unite tho
harmony.

30

Imagination

Imagination is a good thing. To imagine ourselves where we want to go, is wonderful!

The idea is the cradle of deeds, the dynamo of a successful life.

Imagination gives us wings and fills our hearts with courage and faith in our own strength.

Insult

Only petty people think they show their authority by insulting others —

Only the wicked try to lower the self-esteem of other people and spit in their faces.

They spit against the wind!

Interest

Be interested in people; ask where they are from, how they live, how many children they have — whether they are happy, what they read, what are their pleasures.

Read people like you read books — not from curiosity, or idle gossip, but from a desire to learn.

Man is still the most interesting creature under the sun!

Joy

Seneca said, many, many years ago: "Real joy is a serious matter."

Joyfulness

A joyful face is always received kindly. Even the most grumpy and frozen heart will thaw in its presence!

Judgment

Most of the time we are too harsh and quick in our judgments.

"He is a wastrel, a ne'er-do-well, a thief—" But can we prove it?

Did we see it with our own eyes?

Did we stop his hand?

What shall we do if we find we were mistaken?

Key

Remember, there are two keys to human hearts:
"Please" and "Thank you."

Kindness

Whether it be to animal or bird, tree or flower,
— show your good will!

Be kind, do not be hurtful.

One friend of mine talks to plants while watering them, encouraging them to grow better. To those people who cannot be kind on their own, I offer this bit of advice:

"If you want honey, do not kick the beehive."

Laughter

Laugh — not mockingly, sneeringly, cynically, but indulgently, patiently, prudently, and with laughter which does not hurt or insult.

Laughter — honest, sincere, from the depths of a gallant and brave heart, is a blessing.

Letters

We like to receive them, but we do not like to write them!

A letter is a sunbeam on a gray day. A letter is a smile, — a friendly look from one eye to another — a handclasp or sometimes even the opening of a safety valve.

Few people can write a letter, for it is an art even rarer than the art of speech.

When we write a letter we often cease to be natural and we become hypocrites.

"Paper," as Cicero said, "does not blush."

Life

It is possible to live pleasantly without living wisely and justly; and it is impossible to live wisely and justly without living pleasantly.

Most men employ the earlier part of life to make the other part miserable.

The art of living depends ninety percent on how we can get along with people we cannot stand.
SAMUEL GOLDWYN

Human life resembles fire: it begins with smoke and ends with ashes.

All of the animals know that the principal business of life is to enjoy it.
SAMUEL BUTLER JR.

Love

The whole world is suffering. Over all of us lies a fog of mistrust, of uncertainty, of restlessness. We search for something, we hunger. But we hunger more with our souls than with our bodies. We have lost our purpose in life. Where are we going to find it again?

Where shall we find rest and peace? Where is our guiding star? Why are we here; where are we going? We do not know — but we know one thing: we want to be happy! Eternally happy!

This happiness dwells not only in peace of mind; but needs also a shining goal to which we can aspire. For this, we have to have a good compass.

Where is the road? And where is the compass?

There is only one compass and one road: Love.

Love of man for his brother.

Love which does not hurt, offend or humiliate.

Love which understands and forgives, which does not know the difference between classes, nations or races, does not know barriers or castes which separate one man from another.

Love which does not know impatience, but

which waits patiently for his slower comrade to keep up with him.

Love which is the flowering romance of long-deceased knights.

Love which gives us wings!

In most hearts there is a small thorn of hate — we must find another Androcles to take out that thorn! It will be a difficult operation, but it can be done! Where there is infinite patience and infinite love—everything is possible. Everything.

Only through love can we reach other people — it is the only platform on which the whole world can meet — German and Chinese, Japanese and Russian, Indian and Hindu, English and French.

Love is peace and strength.

War and hate are weakness, hazard and rage.

Love is the only language every man understands — it is the best language of all!

Loving

Loving is to be of service.

Service is good business,

Service is profitable,

Loving is profitable!

It is paid for by the happiness in our hearts.

Marriage

To marry well means to find a woman who has two things: First of all, she must be a woman with much, much patience!

Second, she must be a woman who will love you always, who will believe in you and who will walk faithfully at your side throughout life —

Find a sensible woman with good character!

Beauty of soul is more than beauty of body because it does not age.

When a man chooses a good wife, he holds four aces in his hand and he does not need to be afraid to draw a card with courage.   T. H. LORIMER

Mirror

Everybody around us has good characteristics which we would like to have ourselves; and everybody has bad points which we know we have too.

The people around us are our eternal mirrors. When we begin to realize that we share other people's faults, we shall begin to see how we ourselves look to others.

Money

Money is very nice to have, — and it is pleasant to be able to buy many things with it.

But once in a while take an inventory of those things which money cannot buy.

Monotony

Monotony exhausts and ages people.

Let us not forget in our workaday world the beauty all around us. Put a flower in a vase on

your desk — take a walk in the morning — see
the sun rise — smile at the squirrels in the trees,
— the dew on a spider's web — and listen to
the singing of a bird.

Monotony will vanish!

Nations

Nations are proud of their civilization.

How much better it would be if they were proud
of their hearts — this would be *real* civilization!

Not Only I

We must not direct our thoughts only to ourselves. We are not alone in sorrow, nor are we
the only ones who deserve rewards.

Other people have sorrows and work hard, as
well!

Treat people generously and your spirit will
grow.

Offense

If somebody says: "You are stupid," he is either right or he is not.

If he is right, pass it over in silence, to minimize the disgrace of it. Then try to correct your weaknesses.

If he is not right, let him talk. He cannot harm you with his foolish chatter anyway!

Optimism

Life is and always will be a battle.

One must know how to fight it honorably, and not to despair.

It will be found that a healthy optimism is the first guarantee of happiness.

Order

Order in your mind!
Order on your desk!

Order in money matters!

Order in letters!

Order in your work!

Order, order, order! It is like marching to music!

You can march better and more easily to music!

And you can go farther!

Patience

So little patience and love have we for each other! Maybe that is why we are so unhappy.

Or rather, are we so impatient because we are unhappy?

Or is it a vicious circle?

Peace

Peace is one thing we cannot have ourselves unless we give it to others!   ALLEN WHITE

All that is beautiful and noble, all that man has ever kept in his head and heart, is in that one word: Peace!

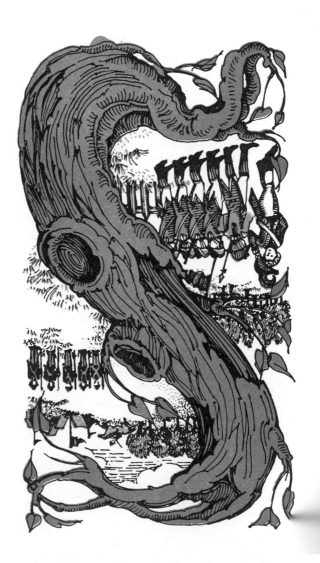

Praise

Do not believe that praise spoils people.

On the contrary, they will try hard to be worthy of the praise.

Praise brings a good rate of interest, — it awakens in a man all that is kind and pleasant — it awakens in him his self-confidence and self-consciousness.

Presence of Mind

"I embrace you, Africa," said the great Roman general Scipio, when after stepping out of a boat on the African coast he stumbled and fell down.

His soldiers would have taken it for a bad omen; but with presence of mind, he turned what might have been a calamity into good fortune!

Risk

Do not be unhappy if you have to change your job or your profession.

Do not be afraid to take a risk. All your life is a risk, — starting nine months before you were born!

Sacrifice

He who is not willing to make sacrifices, is not worthy of love.

Selfishness

Selfishness is a rock on which the best of friendships will suffer shipwreck.

Severity

Let us be strict with ourselves, and thus discourage others from being strict with us.

Admit your faults and errors. It is difficult, even bitter, but it is always healthy!

Slander

They slander those who are silent.

They slander those who speak too much.

They slander those who speak too little.

They slander!

Strength

True strength works slowly,
diligently, day after day,
year after year, without
weariness or exhaustion —
Calm, deep and self-confident.

A strong man does not complain —
only a coward does.

A strong man knows how to wait;
he is not flustered, excited or worn out.

He knows the strength of patient endeavor.

Sunny Side

Even in the worst thunderstorm, to see a blue,
sunny sky ahead and above — that is strength!

Do not let anybody say he spoiled your day.

It has often been said that after a rain, the sun shines more brightly.

Taciturnity

A man came to Alaska at the time of the gold rush, and nobody heard him talk for a whole year. One day he came to the saloon and said: "I found a piece of gold as big as a child's head."

Everybody was surprised that he spoke, for they had all thought he was dumb.

His friends asked him why he had not spoken before, and he answered: "Why, till now I really did not have anything worthwhile to say."

Thanks

We don't know how to say "Thank-you" very well — perhaps we don't want to admit how much we owe to others. But we like to hear the thanks of others,—we sometimes demand them!

Why doesn't the flower called "Thank-you,"
blossom in our garden?

Theatre

We all are actors. We all act — some are better;
some are worse.

Most people act for the benefit of others; some
act even for themselves.

We continually wear masks: sometimes out of
fear or slyness but sometimes because of love
for others.

It is not a sin to put on an act for the benefit of
others — if they cannot take the truth, if their
souls have not yet matured!

Time

There is a banal shopworn saying: "Time is
money."

Time is much more than money; time is life,
time is multitudes of seconds going through the

fingers of the present into the past, . . . moments that will never return.

MEMENTO VIVERE! Don't forget to live! Johann W. Goethe had that motto engraved on his watch.

Today

Today is the son of yesterday —
Today is the father of tomorrow.

Long is yesterday, and long is tomorrow —
So short is today!

Don't let it slip between your fingers.

Let it contain beauty, hope and love, as well as work and rest.

Every day helps decide about us, — about the richness of our wisdom, the tenderness of our hearts, or the fullness of our lives.

Let us not postpone those things which bring us

good; but equally, let us not delay the things which bring us gall, envy and hate.

Our whole life is a chain of our todays.

Tolerance

Only other people are unbearable!

Tolerance! Many qualities repose in this word: kindness and love; magnanimity and modesty; peace and devotion; justice and respect; providence and discipline.

Also wisdom of heart and head!

Training

If I do not practice for one day, I know.

If I do not practice for two days my colleague knows.

If I do not practice for a week — even a layman will know.

VIOLINIST REZNIKOV

Trust

Trust a thief with a purse, and see, he will not disappoint you!

Two

Two is a beautiful number.

One is a number achieved only by one in millions. But two: friends, lovers, mother and child, —the beginning of life, the beginning of strength and love!

Universe

Spread the wings of your spirit from the North Pole to the South Pole and catch the whole splendor of the Universe!

The Universe is yours!

Vacation

Rest after work. Gain new strength.

We must appraise the happenings of the year

behind us; we must gather new hope for the year ahead — we must stop to contemplate a little about ourselves.

Velvet Glove

We must have principles! Let us keep them; but do not force them on others harshly or ruthlessly. Criticism can be made gently, in a friendly and quiet manner, so that others will not be hurt.

Why?

Why do we always want the things we cannot have?

Why do we not avail ourselves of those things which we can have for the asking: the beauty of the countryside, the color of flowers, the magic of snowflakes, the loveliness of clouds passing in the sky above us, the sparkle of the stars shining in the silent night?

Why are we not content with our riches?

Wisdom

A wise man is not grave, stiff and over-serious, but smiling, serene and benign.

He walks on the sunny side of the street and appreciates a good joke.

Nothing spoils his joy of life. With a smile he can congratulate his opponent, and wisely he can joke about himself.

Wrath

Wait; do not get angry! In an hour you will laugh at the whole matter. Cæsar used to count up to a hundred when he was angry. Perhaps twenty should be enough for us?

Count slowly!

Xmas

People are never as kind or as happy as at Christmas time!

He who is kind, has the spirit of Christmas all the year 'round.

Make your life a continual Christmas!

Young in Heart

Life begins at forty!

It does not matter that we have gray hair or wrinkles, as long as the wrinkles are not in our hearts or our souls.

You

You will be shaped by two things: The way in which you behave toward yourself, and the way in which you behave toward other people.

Zest

"Every day, in every way, I feel better and better." This was a little sentence recommended by Emile Coué to be said to oneself morning and evening. Do it! It will put zest in your life!

IN CONCLUSION
MY WISH FOR YOU IS:
GOOD WIND IN YOUR SAILS
SAILOR OF LIFE!

THIS VOLUME
HAS BEEN PREPARED
PRINTED AND PUBLISHED
AT THE OFFICE OF
THE PETER PAUPER PRESS
MOUNT VERNON
NEW YORK